STONY LONESOME

Poems by Kelly Dean Jolley

Library of Congress Control Number: 2014948182

ISBN: 978-0-9857703-5-8

Stony Lonesome, by Kelly Dean Jolley

Published by Summerfield Publishing, New Plains Press

PO Box 1946

Auburn, AL 36831-1946

Newplainspress.com

Dedicated to Ward and Peggy Allen,
to Loxley Compton, to Andy Bass,
and to all my long-suffering students

ACKNOWLEDGEMENTS

I thank Hollie Lavenstein, Keren Gorodeisky, Jeanne Clothiaux, Carly Lane, John Hartsfield and Andy Bass for their encouragement and many useful suggestions. I also thank John Summerfield, New Plains' publisher, for his interest in and support of the book. I also thank the editorial staff of New Plains—they were helpful along many different dimensions.

To my wife, Shanna, and to my children, Eli and Sydney, my love and my thanks, both finally inexpressible, for making mine a life that sustains poetry. I owe to my grandmother, Evelyn Jolley, my lifelong love of words, of their flesh and of their spirit. My parents, Dwayne and Connie Jolley, were willing often to leave me alone with books, a genuine kindness. My father's inwardness with scripture remains my touchstone of bringing words to life.

STONY LONESOME

Πρόσχωμεν!
~The Divine Liturgy

All minds quote.
~Emerson

It is not until we have eaten the apple with which the serpent philosopher tempts us, that we begin to stumble on the familiar and to feel that haunting sense of alienation which is treasured by each generation as its unique possession. This alienation, the gap between oneself and the world, can only be resolved by eating the apple to the core; for after the first bite there is no return to innocence. There are many anodynes, but only one cure. We may philosophize well or ill, but we must philosophize.
~Wilfrid Sellars

TABLE OF CONTENTS

UPHILL

Laboring uphill
unlike Dante
my steps do not lighten
as I go

Pine pollinates
shoes a dusty green
olive drab slightly yellowed

Alive between Inferno
and Paradise
Purgatory
we may sin no more
but we pay for the sins
behind and below us

Seven cursive P's
wound my forehead
peccati
one for each day
my weak

We rent a cabin
on the hill
looking down
on water

Prayers from those
breathing, casting shadows
sporting their Adam or Eve
could shorten my time
uphill

I follow a path
trees marked Passover red
run my hand along the bark

where fire chased these trees
scorched their ankles

Atop the hill
a Lodge
closed for repairs
statework taking its
sweet overtime

How can they leave it closed
with so many waiting to enter
and stay?

Life: serious in strange ways
Immanent, transcendent
betwixt, bewitched, between
inexperience facing
demands of the day

Uphill laboring
by footfalls

I am callow
unable to focus
upon life's liturgy
its seriously play
unwilling to accept
it as a gift
so misunderstanding
it as a task

Love loves
hopes to love understandingly
but loves misunderstandingly
often
making unhappy
lover and beloved

I do not have my life
in precise and stringent categories
sloughed in sloppy thinking
wringing lilies from acorns
chasing rabbits on oxen
out of season
even in season

Can we be poesy
can we live metered lives
can we find ourselves Canting
day to day
turning to the left
to find Virgil there, whenever?

It is our vacation
the family's
holiday

I would dignify my leisure
taking time to sorrow
in knowing
no one crowned
or mitered me Lord
of myself
too impure, too flabby
to mount to the stars

I labor uphill
my forehead a child's
penmanship lesson

READING HUSSERL, OR WANDERING ABOUT THE PANOPTICUM WAXWORKS

For my phenomenology students

I have been reading
Husserl

I think
it is hard to tell

to tell the difference

between reading
and seeing

his pages

I confront them
sternly receptive
hoping for a clear sentence

one that will carry clarity a little further
and make the page more than a motley of wanton arabesques

I need for my intuitive presentation
of the physical appearance of the words
to undergo an essential phenomenological modification
(that's rather a mouthful)
so that the words count as expressions
(Mean something, dammit!)
and I can understand
enliven the waxworks

my meaning intentions cry out
for meaning fulfillments

For the earnest expectation of the creature
Waiteth for the manifestation of the sons of God

Reading well
I hear
is reading true books
in a true spirit—a noble exercise

but here I am
in a sweat
reminding myself: no pain, no gain
lifting long sentences weighted with imponderable German
the unintelligible lite-ness of being-Husserl
And it may be
that the books of
the great poets have
yet to be read, and that because
only a great poet can read them

And so it may be
at least by that math
that I am no great phenomenologist

I haven't as many
eyes
as Husserl

I have only the one

LITTLE LUSTRUM

Tear up
your banalities
Pawkwin
tear up

ALABAMA PITS

Weedowee
Alabama
Pit bulls
anchored fast
to prone
barrels
up and down
the sides
of the hollow

Extra-ordinary
dogs
capable of
a canine
podvig
left untutored
in a canine
gulag
an Archipelago
linked by heavy
chains

Brindle
coats
red and chocolate
left outside
as livestock

Unkillers
rather gladiators
unfazed by
governing children

Upright we
sires and bitches
two-legged

confuse the body
with flesh

Southern
hounds bear
deep scars
teeth-carved
in hide

Body, Flesh, Blood:
we require
them to live
by Cajun rules
while we cheat

Queequeg, remember,
Queequeg dies game
so said Pip
it is a mutual
joint-stock world
in all meridians
these dogs
could help us men

Child
and dog
in virtue's embrace
both smile
forgotten photo

Scratch
unanswered

ALICE
(An Anti-Tate Poem)

Alice,
once a logician's fetish
is no longer little Alice
she is old, and fat;
cannot fit through the looking-glass

Alice,
life grown small
no draught can enlarge it
sentence first, verdict afterwards;
how final now the sentence
as she overhears the verdict

Alice,
she would be tardy,
for an important date
but shall be prompt
for it is always death
today, and not tomorrow;

Jam's gone
Goodnight, Alice

ON THE EVE OF THE END

On the eve of the end, the Mayan-made end of all things

I sit and drink coffee, writing and reading, unwilling to meet coming darkness
sleepy with unmarked pages

On the eve of the end, the Mayan-made end of all things

I sit and notice that no one seems to worried, really, unable to see the dark
comet hurtling at us

Invisible, uncoated with ice and stone, heaven's stealth weapon

On the eve of the end, the Mayan-made end of all things

I sit and wonder if I should have outgrown my Mayan stage in junior high,
counting vigesimally

—we are at about 5 in our countdown from 20 to nothing-at-all, a real zero

On the eve of the end, the Mayan-made end of all things

I sit and ponder Max Stirner, who set his cause on nothing, and consider what
he would have thought

since both his ego and his own, and all the hell else, are about to be naugh-
ted, regardless of whether they are naughty or nice (Christmas Apocalypse,
Dec 21)

*I have been so naughted in Thy Love's existence that my nonexistence is a
thousand times sweeter than my existence:* Rumi said that, and I have stood
where he did, and looked up

at his turquoise dome beneath the azure Turkish sky,
the latter about to darken and the former about

to fall

On the eve of the end, the Mayan-made end of all things

I sit

I wait

I expect

nothing

CURTAINS OF RAIN

Rain runs heavy to ground
the sky a cheap grey colander
outside

Our front window
curtains open
reveal the window
the sheers behind the curtains
in front of the window

The sheers are snagged, torn
hose with runners, up-down, left-right
a cat's favor

The sheers are half-open
I can see the rain through them
see it without them
through the window

I suppose the sheers should be closed
or open or anyway not half-and-half
if we respected ourselves I suppose
we'd replace them with sheers without runs

But these are our sheers, so disposed
not disposed of, kept half-open
with runners

And this is our life together in this house
half-open, with runners
unsheerly concealing, sheerly revealing
the curtains pulled back
inside

LEAVING MAYBERRY

Death paid a call
last night
dropped in unexpected
we weren't receiving visitors

Andy Griffith was on tv
at first we didn't notice
Death's tuneless quiet whistle

But when Barney said
"Nip it! Nip it! Nip it in the bud!"
Death stopped whistling
all we could hear
was silence and Death
rocking in his chair

We knew someone was headed
to Mt. Pilot

BIJ MIST

Eliot had his Ash Wednesday,
but I had his Thursday, Friday, Saturday, Sunday, Monday, Tuesday
and a Wednesday of my own

Volcanic ash farted
some unnameable Icelandic volcano (April 2010)
grounds flyers

In the UK, intending no prophecy, I quote Hecuba's words as the ash cloud
drifts
south and east:
        Nunc trahor exul, inops

Clouds of unknowing
reveal my deordinate self—
anxiety quietly unmans me

Aboard a bus, a coach
on a carriage-way,
13 hours, Manchester to Amsterdam
        white tulips in a lamplit English village
        stretch and harden into white cliffs at Dover
we ferry to Calais

Conferring in Crewe
take-away northern industrial village
ordinary language (philosophy)
in a place consternatingly plain

No pile of Galaxy chocolate
can sweeten this ashy mess
nothing colligates these loose ends

        Get me off this English roundabout

Oh, Eliot!
> *Teach us to care and not to care;*
> *teach us to sit still*
> *even among these ashes,*
> *our peace in his will*
—Not so much

THE CARE AND FEEDING
OF WILLIAM FAULKNER

William Faulkner visits Iceland in the early 50's

Faulkner's coming
   Here, to Iceland
We're to show him a good time
   But, not too good
In Japan, he misbehaved badly
   Drunk, on hard stuff
We should serve him beer
   Just, not too much
Keep a constant careful eye on him
   Slightly, on his glass

"Doesn't anyone here drink hard liquor?"
William, William
meet our guests

Don't you want to meet the famous authors of Iceland?
Here's one who may win a Nobel prize, like you
bring it back to the ice and snow and boiling waters
like you did to the sun and heat and gentle warm springs
(Silence)
Too bad you don't say much—at least you don't talk about yourself

The State Department sent you to Iceland
to convince them that we, we Americans
are worth knowing, worth having around

Your job is to show them our culture; and you can do that by just
being there, by sharing your high and nobel presence
we write, too, and read
true, we have to keep a watch on our culture
it drinks, you know, bourbon on the rocks in a tall glass
gets wobbly, we have to send cablegrams
addressed to the one Southerner in all of Iceland,
explaining the care and feeding of our culture
since (sometimes) it cannot stand on its own

KNEED

Sometimes, Apple, my knees are too much with me
        cartilage sandy and stringy

I am unbowed, my knees unbending
        but not from any upright unyielding

If I were to kneel, I could not get up
        Apple, both you and I decay

BEGRIFFSSCHRIFT

In poetry, we have the case of thoughts being expressed without being actually put forward as true in spite of the form of the indicative sentence, although it might be suggested to the hearer to make an assenting judgment himself. Therefore it must still always be asked, about what is presented in the form of an indicative sentence, whether it really counts as an assertion. And this question must be answered in the negative if the requisite seriousness is lacking. [1]

[to the reader]

I.

Gottlob Frege invented it,
yes, let's say he invented it,
his ideography

His formula language
modeled on that of arithmetic
for pure thought

J. L. Austin, who turned Frege's German English classically
termed it "concept writing"
that is what I call it too

For Frege, it is a language,
a way of writing indifferent to anything
that is itself indifferent to argument, to truth, to truth values

The True and The False

It cares only for content
Begrifflichen Inhalt
One word as good as another if truth is untouched

If it is one of the tasks of philosophy to break the domination of the word over the human spirit by laying bare the misconceptions that through the use of language almost

unavoidably arise concerning the relations among concepts by freeing them from that
with which only the means of expression of ordinary language, constituted as they are,
saddle it, then my ideography...can become a useful tool for the philosopher. [2]

Yes, it is one of the tasks of philosophy
to break the domination of the word
over the human spirit
to battle against the bewitchment
of the intellect by means of language

But Frege did not know
maybe he could not know or could not but refuse to know
that this is one of the tasks of poetry too
Although I admit it does not seem to be
it is as though it is poetry (peculiarly poetry)
in which words most dominate the human spirit

Most completely bewitch the intellect
lulling it into a dreamy slumber
talking it into taking a holiday
inducing an idled-engine, shaky stillness

But if we reflect
we will see we have nothing
to battle language with but
more language

And though we may, as Chapman hoped
open poesy by poesy
we may also combat poesy by poesy
knowing that the word
a two-edged sword
quick, powerful, capable of turning on itself
discerning its own thoughts, intents
dividing asunder sign and significant use

Because the strangeness of the human spirit
is that it can only be dominated by what expresses it
say, by its own expressions, each word a potential sentencing
But Frege, wonderful Frege!, partly sagacious in Jena
struggling to free the human spirit even while his own
remained locked in a cell of spasmodic hatefulness
(the Democrats, the French, the Catholics, the Jews!);
but still, wonderful Frege!, —few find the way, the narrow way,
to liberation, but fewer still those who find the way-end

II.

*It is just as important to neglect distinctions that do not touch the heart of the matter
as to make distinctions which concern what is essential. But what is essential depends
on one's purpose. To a mind concerned with what is beautiful in language what is
indifferent to the logician can appear as just what is important.* [3]

Frege blanched at poetry, no surprise;
he saw no difference between
'horse', 'steed', 'cart-horse', 'mare'
believing that the choice made no difference to truth

But that's false, since (we know) it is true
that Robert E. Lee rode a horse but false
he rode a mare—and if you are buying your own
war-horse, it would be true
that you want a steed but false
that you want a cart-horse

Frege can respond
that if you confront
a female horse pulling
a cart
you can say

"She's a horse", or "She's a steed" or
"She's a cart-horse" or even "She's a mare"
and we, if we are willing not to chivvy

might say, "True" to each alike; yes, Frege
can so respond, but now he allows referent
to determine sense,
or anyway makes apparent that he has lived
in the absence of horses

[to Frege]

III.

Poems, I say, as did F. R. Leavis
exist neither on the page nor in individual minds
but in a *Third Realm*, a term, Frege, that you
and Leavis both reached for out of different
but related needs

Poems exist not in minds but in the Mind

You did not know the hammer-and-chisel logic
of a George Oppen poem or the eidectic splendor
of a poem by William Carlos Williams

If you say, "But that's not *logic*!", fine;
but it is not psychology either
call it "grammar", call it "phenomenology"
after all, so much depends on how one holds an apple
on a red wheel barrow—
and no poem floats in a psychological washtub

Poetry reveals the essence of conscious states,
presentative, judgmental, desiderative; it shows
the essential structure of moods; it teaches us how
objects enter into our experience

Poetry teaches our moods to believe in each other

IV.

You, Frege, wonderful Frege!, reckon that poems
have their aim revealed by beauty, not truth;
you hold that writing for beauty
is not serious, and thus you contend even that
the indicative structure of poetry is fraudulent, you
deem their indicative structure a failure to assert
that has the form of an assertion, as if poems had the form
of assertion but denied the power thereof

I guess I understand that
but seriousness itself is often fraudulent,
and there are options for seriousness other than
non-seriousness, frivolity

Poetry allows us to see by helping us recognize
all that we live through when we see, and if it does so
best by emanating from a disinterest that Eckhart
would admire, it offers the kingdom of the world we live in
as the fulfillment of its poverty of spirit

(Writing poetry we want nothing, know nothing, have nothing,
not even the poem; we write out of the most intimate poverty discoverable)

it does what it does without our needing to or being able to say
how it does it: there is no need to understand how

Poetry washes the fur without wetting it

And maybe that is the rub, Frege? Maybe it is that in poetry
truth is behind us, as ἀρχή, and not before us, as τέλος,
that makes poetry make you uneasy, maybe understanding
beauty as aim makes poetry seem responsive only to the laws of beauty, as
if it were indifferent to truth as concept-writing was for you indifferent to
beauty, --maybe that is what requires that you place it, put it in its place

—but wrongly, or not exactly rightly

Poetry chases beauty, but the chase succeeds
When the chaser runs soothfast

Poetry too is concept-writing

[to the reader]

V.

The meaning of a word
is its use in the language
at least for a large number of cases (Wittgenstein)

Do those cases include the case of poetry?
Some say not (O. K., Bouwsma), but why?
Surely words are used in poetry, and even if
they are used in ways that strain or crack or
metaschematize their use in prosaic language
disturbing or dispensing their trailing clouds of etymology,
their meaning here is a function of their meaning there—
the act of meaning them now is founded on acts of meaning them then

But we want, not just Frege, but all of us, in certain frames
of mind we want desperately to use words in ways that free us
from all the troubles of words;
as Merleau-Ponty said: *We all secretly venerate*
the ideal of a language which in the last analysis
would deliver us from language
by delivering us to things

Deliver us from the evils of words
save us from verbal adventures
deliver us whole and mute to the silence of things

But things are not silent—they just cannot speak
And they keep their counsel not because they are reticent
but because they know no better, knowing nothing

And a *Begriffsscchrift*, logical or poetical, cannot free
itself from the troubles of words;
ideal language is language still

Words perplex words

SUNBAKE

Burn
Auburn burn
           sunbake redclay
           sunbake

The sun doesn't peer
         it stares
              and stares

no one dares return its glare

We crouch behind colored lenses
         sunbake photogrey
         sunbake

You look to the sun, for he is your taskmaster
and by him you know the measure of the work
you have done, and he measure of the work
that remains for you to do: thus Kinglake

My daughter, ten or eleven
child of memory, eternally clear: "Dad, it's hot"

She hankers for ice cream
         sunbake icecream
         sunbake

Cooled by the malt
           of mercy

LECTURER (PAUSING)

Do I teach to lend an ear (Samuel to God) or to give the eye (Saul to David)
obey or suspect, exhort or dehort, build or burn
I prophesy a new hearkening
I chant the gassing of structures of air

Chalk in hand I am poised to move on, to talk more
to ask questions whose answers I do not know but
whose interrogation of myself I cannot resist, students wonder
but I cannot help asking: I have time to fill
(Monday, Wednesday, Friday at 2—post meridian)
and I have to fill time—bruise eternity but leave it living

> *If you cannot cover a question with words*
> *you let it ask you too much*

Out of what dustbin of mine draw I fresh water
out of what fancy of mine produce I plain help
to insist on the difference between me and them:
me, not young but clever
them, not clever but young:
insisting on this would be false, but worse treats an accident
as fated, as if learning weighed a few ounces
in the balance of a new testament

Simple faith simply is the only faith there is
and whatever tincture of complication or sophistication
enters into denatures it completely, even if it seems natural still
students wonder faithfully and I am finical over that faith
fearful that I only complicate or sophisticate, sophists' accomplice

To teach is to unlearn, forget, desert
what I have it in me to teach
I do not know, I know, I do not know
but known ignorance is not my Socratic crux
not my particular poison

M'occorreva il coltello che recide
la mente che decide e si determina

I dust chalky hands against my pants and worry
students wander at their desks
chalk in hand I am poised to move on

GERTRUDE STEIN BLUES

Sat me down sad and heavy
Sat me down plus and minus
Sat me down bond and bail
Sat me down yours and mine

Sat me down sad and heavy
Sat me down write and rhyme
Sat me down *hic et nunc*
Sat me down rock and roll

Sat me down sad and heavy
Sat me down son and daughter
Sat me down white and black
Sat me down tender buttons

Sat me down sad and heavy
Sat me down sad and
Sat me down sad
Sat me down
Sat me
Sad

A COUNTING

Sun on sand
and sand holding loosely old footprints
(a breeze could break the grip)

And from one
point of view I am those footprints
sunned, benighted; sunned, benighted
until the breeze comes
and the sand lets go
of me—dust to the wind

A wife (mine) walks to the rising sun
on her way somewhere three-dimensional
length and breadth and height and depth
(is that four dimensions?)
while I remain in my pulpy inky flatland
the two dimensions of success or failure

I am called to accountancy
an accountancy of living
(Thoreau called it 'philosophy')
that makes what I reckon
as my life

And I must keep the books
even as the black bleeds into red
and even as the columns quiver
(eyeless in a paper Gaza)

Why count the cost of these things?

Because there is no natural number
all I can do is to count on these things,
live with their cost

THE PHENOMENON OF WATER

We see ourselves in water.

What do we know about water? I don't mean: it's H2O. I mean, what do we know about it? What is water? It is hot (steam), wet (liquid) and solid (ice). It changes. We drink it but cannot grasp it, although it leaves evidence of its escape in our hands.

We are mostly water; we know this as we might blindly countersign a statement: but we experience it, really know it, when we are athirst, deeply athirst, and when our need for water shows itself as a need to reconstitute ourselves. Our thirst can be deep and gorgeous, and we can drink so greedily that water overflows our gulping and spills down our cheeks, darkening our shirts. We long for oases in the deserts of our lives with a longing so strong that we see oases even where they are not, mirages of water, seemingly made of water, liquid, mobile, shimmering: the satisfaction of thirst displayed in glowing waterlogged green before the dessicated eye of the mind.

We cry tears of water. We are water houses. Our sorrows wring our water from us. We liquefy sadness; our hearts pump water from our eyes. But we also liquefy joy. Tears bedew smiles, they can appear on the upcast visage. Our deepest emotions show in water.

We waste water. It goes through us and then out of us, taking impurity with it. It bathes us, outside and inside. We make water.

We play in water. Swim. Float. Dive. Drown. We find it at the end of a plank or sink into it as our ship goes down. It is fathomless. It houses the Leviathan and provides a moving platform for Ahab's Titanic hatred. On water, we seek the weather gage and steer by the stars. We know ourselves little then and our comforts, like Ahab's pipe, seem no longer comforting. The sea moves in mysterious ways. It claims the dead but occasionally lends them to shore. Salt water threatens as sweet water does not, as if the salt itself were an admixture of corruption, an alien leavening that turns the water on us. Our lives are a sea, and we float upon it, clutching a casket, our own. We can each say: Call me Ishmael. We wander the watery parts of the world.

Water reveals the mind. Aristotle calls the mind the formless place of the forms. Water is like that. Liquid, it assumes the form of whatever contains it. It has no natural shape, no shape of its own; and this is why it can assume so many shapes. Like water, if still too long, the mind becomes stagnant. Our mind needs to run.

Water is holy. We are baptized in it, as was Christ, from whose side would run blood and water at the finish of his crucifixion. Our baptism redeems us. Christ's baptism redeemed the waters, Theophany waters. Warmed, as *zeon*, water represents our religious fervor, zeal, and reminds us that the Body of which we partake is the warm body, the resurrection body. We bless the water and the water blesses us.

We see ourselves in water.

SPRING

Beneath a Bartlett pear
upright in its spring candor
a judgmatic plum grows
grasping upward with spread fingers
delicately dotted in warm pink

Birdsong garlands the empty spaces
of the yard as the afternoon
sunlight stretches to retain
its ubiquitous gloze

I sit on the edge
of the yard—in it but
not of it—wearing
no bridal garment

My clothing accuses me:
black shirt and grey pants
black socks and shoes, a
chromatic color amiss:
but my eyes are blue

CROWNS

A mock curtsey
in a coffee shop
a clatch of young women
in the space of a smile
talking, oddly,
of heavenly crowns
and their weight

I DREAMT A JUMBLE OF THINGS.
THEN ALL TIDIED ITSELF

Muffled light of a sanctuary lamp
eyes now open, large and dark,
moments before closed, hidden
vestigial tremors near the call into being
out of an unbeing cleaved to closely

I dreamt a jumble of things
a worded page stretching from
visual periphery to visual periphery
a sentence, choose one!, as horizon
hemmed in by dreamy palaver
meaning everything, meaning nothing
at once and earlier and later

Conscious now, the words linger
or their senses do, without reference
the meanings present absences
de re Nonsenses, *de rerum natura*
when will words again be word,

                                    i.e., Word
utterly words, so to speak,
when will everything that can be said be said
clearly? (I'd settle if someone whistled a
snatch for me)

Everything's smutched, jumbled,
dreamt words tell me no more than I knew
as I slept. In a dreamy sentence Bachelard
prophesied: *the words of the world want to make
sentences.* I believe it, and against my dream
all tidies itself: the words gather in the morning, crowd
together between periods—together now, at least in twos
(noun and verb), they make sense, couple

Loud sunlight overspeaks the sanctuary lamp
the horizon is now visible, neither intelligible
nor unintelligible
I arise reassured of something—I know not what
I am rooted in
an old faith, the jumbled-made-tidy,
I walk by reading and not by sight

OBJECTIVITIES

Rereading Berryman's dreamsongs
reminded of how self-loathing
purchases a kind of objectivity
    —and there are kinds, you know,
    not just one kind of objectivity
    but rather objectivities,
        kind and unkind
    to mention two

Our kind of objectivity these days,
a consuming kind,
the objectivity of hundreds of choices
spreadeagled on an internet page
    —click to buy

Pound sang, croaked, of usura and sure he
may have been cracked
but he foreknew our usury of ourselves
and each other
    —seeing in each other not
    the image and likeness of God
    but of Mammon
        de eyes de pricetag of de soul,
        son, say Mr. Bones.

OUT OF THE PAST

1. Jane Greer looks frankly into the camera
wearing a black negligee, 1946
laced about with smoke
from her cigarette

looking from out of the past

Robert Mitchum in a raincoat
in a darkened city
enshadowed by longing
and all his regret

Longing from out of the past

> And you wonder where you come from
> How can the days all be the same?
> And you wonder where you come from
> And why your name's your name

2. Build my gallows high, babe
dangle me from an ebon tree
I hang from all I've done
or I hang for all I've done

No one is righteous, no

Not once have I sat
in a South American cantina
wrapped in a brown study
waiting for a woman,

For Jane Greer,
who would have been worth it all,
the bullet in the gut,
even the car crash at the end

But I want to make a break
to pass on the past

What has history to do with me?
mine is the first and only world

     Because the past is not always
     a mode of access to what's real
     and the things you felt in childhood
     need not thematize what you feel

Looking, longing, running
you wonder where you came from

LEAVINGS

New Orleans
city to walk in
so a city to write poetry in

The streets are poetry
Toulouse
St. Louis

Music tie-dyes the air
neon

Heard on the street (one man yelling to another)
—Can you make the sun shine?
—Yes, but it is a six-week process!

A woman leans weightlessly against a door   Galatoire's
her dress quintessence
her skin pink alabaster
black hair and violet eyes
(a bayou Vivian Leigh)

Another woman sings jazz bravely
in the shadow of Irma Thomas' statue

Overcast February Saturday
damp beignets
powdered sugar coats a child's cheeks
some spilled on the ground
sweet sorrowful leavings

A little hard
to say goodbye
to the Big Easy

FEBRUARY 22

Walking sticks
four

Each of us
walking and talking
pond and shadows
frogs and
sticks

four

Each of us
three
generations

Each embued with energy

God's

      God didn't make me rich
      but he made ends meet
      what do you think of that?

Tithing, telling tales

Working on manners
our own

Thinking of ourselves no more
than we ought

frogs mumble
we see things in the rippled water
we cannot see above it

IN THE DISTANCE

In the distance I saw
a girl, slim and small, green eyes
and braided hair

And I loved her then--
maybe I didn't know it,
but my bones did, and my eyes;
my mind is always last to know.

She was in the distance, across
a large room,
dressed in a light turquoise dress
and white shoes

Eventually, reckless and anxious,
I asked her out in muttered stages:
"Do you know who I am?"
"Do you find me radically offensive?"
"Will you go out with me?"

She answered:
"Yes"
"No"
and "How old are you?"

Then, relieved and suave
(as I thought),
I answered:
"I'm not as old as I am"

Yes, nonsense, that
but as is often true in the times of
crucial experiment in our lives,
we bridge from one understanding
of who we are to another via some paradox
or other, some unintended oracle

For indeed I am not as old as I am still,
just as I wasn't then, in the distance of the past,
and the woman whose life interpenetrates mine,
who is as much the author and finisher of all I have done
as I am, synergistically, my lover and fellow-worker,
has lived with me, and lived with me, for these many years

I still stand before her as I did then, hat in hand,
overcoated against the world, flustered, and inarticulate--
lost and found in the distance of my own thoughts, talking
nonsense when I should be not be talking

But, as she did then, she smiles at my mumuration,
bids me back
to her, to all that we have been and are
and shall be together,
as it all trisects the extended present

Today
I recall the advent of her
in the distance

WALKING GRAVEYARDS

Three years in the grave
his Beatrice beloved
her stone still unlettered

Knew no words to save
their love as uncorrupted
his bed ill-comforted

for three years
he walked graveyards
funereal reading
tracing carved letters
with aged fingers
eyes now failing

Grief enough to rave
against the stones untended
love lives indentured

       Maybe words tomorrow

for three years
he walked graveyards
funereal reading

Her stone still
unlettered

THE CIGARETTE TREE
For Andy Bass

In the midst of the Garden
there is a Cigarette Tree
I stop by it sometimes
pick its fruit,

    Getting a light from the Angel with the flaming sword,
    overkill, I know, but no matches grow anywhere and I have no light
    but I keep hoping for knowledge of good and evil,
    I keep hoping for more to say for myself, something to say for myself
    when God stops by in the menthol cool of the evening,
    finds me smoking, smiling a knowing smile,
    A smile I learnt from the serpent, who first urged me to pluck fruit
    from the Cigarette Tree, lucky strike.
    —Although it was a woman who led me to the fruit, and who
    first got me to take a puff. So whose fault was that? She kept telling me
    she'd come a long way and that I would be her Marlboro man.
    (I still don't know what any of that means.)
    I reckon I will be cast out of the Garden: I will end up east of the Tree.
    the Angel won't help me then; the flames will bar my return. And I
    will earn my bread by the sweat of my brow and the woman's childbirth
    will be attended by grief: and the butts of my final cigarettes will breadcrumb
        my path from paradise

LUKE
For Ward Sykes Allen

In a rocker
on the porch of the Overseer's House
behind Stony Lonesome antebellum mansion
he overlooks a new century morning

Beside him
on a table matching his rocker
an open copy of the Authorized Version
his mind submissive and awake to dawn sunlight
        In the treetops

He has no abiding city
living as he does on the farm
his earthly country
a place of horses, whole horses,
        not half-horses, abstracted into horsepower

        They will come no more
        these old men with beautiful manners
        they will come no more

        ("He'd stand up if even a dog came in the room.")

He sits
In peace, knowing how
to go out and come in
even in this, this so busy century

Mindful images
the concrete series of his own history
and his people's—he knows
where he comes from
belongs where he is

The sunlight in the treetops is treacherous,
as all of nature can be
but he will not let creation groan without
engaging it in a dialogue of comfort;
he knows more than he says

Rocking
on the edge of eternity
the sky open above him
waiting
patient

JUDAS

Judas puckered up then plunged down
to potter's field, Aceldama

Hail, Master
Master, Master

The price of blood
left hanging, not for long, he fell headlong
(rope snapped?)
desolated his habitation
by transgression fell

The lot fell, not Judas, on Matthias, who was numbered
twelfth (eleventh and then one)
while Judas hit bottom, no bounce, burst
burst asunder in the midst
(middle popped?)

His bowels moved unmercifully
gushed out
reward of iniquity

Was his guilt heavy
did it account for his headlong fall, his bursting, his gushing?
he was thirty pieces of silver lighter
but that pucker
that kiss
that kiss was weighty
weightier than the silver that bought it

He died (fell headlong)
kissed the dirt
dirt he bought
for kissing

FOOTPATH AND RUNWAY

When we walk with the Lord

stumbling
along, words lightening my feet
pondering their path

rainy Chicago
airport tarmac baptized iridescent black
delayed from 1:43 to 2:08 pm

stewardess gesticulates
her boredom
oxygen is flowing even if
the plastic bag does not fully inflate

Who knew my feet would take me here?
Who knew that following footsteps would lead
me here?

other men, smarter and more solidly educated
talk to me but I know my place
even if bootless ambition makes it pinch

I resolve to turn my back on old goals
even if my hankering
makes me
crane 'round,

Lot's wife, to see my past destinations shrink
reversing their direction
I reorient myself

What a glory He sheds on our way

I have chosen the sheep's life
by choosing the Shepherd
but I have not chosen unreason

I choose to be a Logical sheep
a sheep of the Logos

Plane stalled on the runway almost to take-off
yellow signs order drivers to yield to aircraft
wings matter now, having them, or not

MUDDY WATERS

Muddy waters hide creatures beneath. We know this because
turtles spy on us from nearby, black heads breaking the surface

Each of us, book in hand, sits and reads. We were here last night
when a knot of toads and an army of frogs barked at us, each other
bats frantic twilight butterflies

I think of Modern Love, egoist that I am. I drink the pale drug of
silence, a junky. Forty-one and tongue-tied I have words only
of quotation. Thoreau. Nature exhibits herself to us by turns and
the ice in your pint jar of water falls forward in a clump
against your lip as you drink

No one disturbs us here, although I did hear voices—over there,
by the waterfall. I circle words on the page. 'Mystics', 'depths',
'under'. I etch marginalia: "The holiness of what ought to be?"

Warm in the sun I shut the book. Walk? Yes. We walk in Love's
Deep Woods. I would talk, but the weight of my bag, with our books,
the warmth of the air, shorten my breath

From where this long silence, this big quiet? Who set this watch
on my lips? Will no angel roll back the stone? What seek the speaking
with the dead? The tongue no man can tame time has.

We were here last night. We are here today. We are walking, now
past the waterfall and the knee-high longleaf pines. Trees that have
evolved fire proof. The Barn Trace our path and we end among stones
once a walkway. The house is gone but the barn stands. Silence
is broken by passing cars: We are out of the woods

FOOTNOTES:

[1] Frege, G. "The Thought: A Logical Inquiry", Mind Vol. 65, No. 259, July 1956.

[2] Frege, G. Begriffsschrift in van Heijenoort, J., ed. Frege and Gödel: Two Fundamental Texts in Mathematical Logic (Cambridge, Mass: Harvard University Press, 1970).

[3] "The Thought".

AFTERWORD

Although the poems in this book do not form a sequence, in the technical sense of that term, they are not simply separate poems. Many were written on or written about the wooded paths on the farm, Stony Lonesome, near my home. And that place provides more than a locale of composition or a common thematic element: it radiates a mood in which many, if not all, of the poems participate. –It is not just persons, but also places, that have their moods. The moods of places are subtler but more constant than the moods of persons. Like wind on stone, the moods of places shape the persons who dwell in them. The *genius loci* of Stony Lonesome had a hand on my pen.

These poems quarrel with the Ancient Quarrel between philosophy and poetry. Since these are poems, you may take my side in that quarrel to be decided; but that would be too quick. First, these poems *quarrel* with the Quarrel, and thus do not simply take sides in the Quarrel. Second, these poems quarrel with the *Quarrel*, and thus acknowledge that for two sides to be rightfully said to Quarrel, they must most of the time be on good terms with one another. Many of these poems attempt to suss out, and to show, what those good terms are—to find a way back to the proper converse of philosophy and poetry.

We inhabit what is left of Christendom, and not much is left. We have become secular people, partial people; we no longer believe in, much less live in the interpenetration of the natural and the supernatural: we have lost that sense of mystery that creates ceremony, that reveals to us the garden of the world we live in. In our loss of that sense of mystery, we have lost what galvanizes us against sloth, prevents our souls from growing woolly and fungous. Without mystery, nothing stirs us. We succumb slowly to disrelish and inappetence and unhope. Blind to the seasons' gifts, numb to nature, to human nature and divine nature, careless of ourselves and of others, bored alike by damnation and salvation, we become graceless by inaction. It is one (one) aim of poetry to recover that sense of mystery, to beckon us from sloth.

> ~ *K. D. J.*
> Auburn, Alabama
> July, 2014

Made in the USA
Middletown, DE
03 October 2022

11794542R00043